Turbulence

poems by

Quincy Whitney

Finishing Line Press
Georgetown, Kentucky

Turbulence

Publisher: Leah Maines

Editor: Christen Kincaid

Cover Art: © agsandrew/Depositphotos

Author Photo: Eli Whitney

Cover Design: Gabe, Luke and Keiji of Words From The Woods in Portland,
Maine.

Illustration: "Root Cause," © Gabriel Whitney.

Order online: www.finishinglinepress.com
            also available on amazon.com

Author inquiries and mail orders:
Finishing Line Press
P. O. Box 1626
Georgetown, Kentucky 40324
U. S. A.

Table of Contents

To Eli,
Poet and Poet at Heart—and the Love of My Life.

Special thanks
Alfred Nicol and Rhina Espaillat,

Luminary Poets whose keen insights
are matched only by their kindness—
invaluable mentors and great friends!

A Compass Rose

Solstice

Lingering shadows greet the longest day.
The veil between two worlds is worn away.
The spirits dance, edge near the great divide,
conjuring up the dance of sun inside.

In the shadows of Stonehenge, the hour stops still,
age-old bluestones hauled up a hallowed hill—
stone remnants, sentries marking sacred ground,
haunted by mysteries that still confound.

The sun moves north its canopy of light,
the solstice waits—a hummingbird in flight—
as hard to grasp as a fluttering of wings:
the hour holds the summary of things.

Shadows loom, stretch out the longest of our days,
reminding us too soon that nothing stays.

Rainbow Birch

White is the sum of all colors—
blue, red, yellow, orange, purple, green—
so the white birch may be not white at all
       but a rainbow in disguise.

Molecules float all around us,
paint splatters suspended in mid-air,
       held in place by an invisible web,
a field of energy pulsing.

Like that field we do not see,
so the colors washed by rain,
       the wash of color
remains visible only to those
       who recognize
          the contradiction
             of color and parchment.

Parchment peeling, layers of white,
sheaths of color, layers of paint,
       bark scraps left for writing,
          scrawled messages without words.

Maple's Song

Born on a sunny, sugar maple day
when scarlet maples beckon you to stay,
October sun makes greenness disappear,
and Maple sings her song like a balladeer.
Conceived up north where red maples blow
before Canada's hills fill up with snow,
Maple thrives in the cold, sleet, snow, rain,
dappling red from Minnesota to Maine.
She keeps a rainbow hidden deep inside
then hurls surprise across the mountainside.
On hillside palettes where colors have bled,
only green maples merge purple and red.
Each day, Maple's song brings something new
so hillsides form a psychedelic view.
A quick frost, damp fog, wet spring—anything—
can change the way that Maple's colors sing,
weaving time, space and colors till they dance;
her wildest shades happen when change meets chance.
Orange turns cherry and lime fuses rose—
Maple flashes joy wherever she goes!
Kaleidoscopic colors, wild and free,
form Maple's crazy autumn tapestry.
Maple's palette holds every single hue—
spontaneous, resilient, bold and true.

NOTE: First published in *The Telegraph*, Nashua, New Hampshire, November 22, 2018.

A Compass Rose

Seeing the world through murky glass, a bee—
though blind to color—sees disparity.
Red flowers seem black in gardens grey—
but pattern pulses and pinpoints the way.
When spirals, trumpets, bells and domes align
with serpentine curves of flower design
and craft the sweet targets where nectar flows—
the daisy's pattern turns a compass rose.
Flowers' designs are alphabets of shape—
bullseye tapestries in the bee's landscape—
talismans that mark gardens with ease.
Pinwheel honeysuckle draws honeybees,
as do star-shaped clematis hexagons
and sunflowers' radial lexicons,
while tall filigree towers of foxglove
call to bumblebees hovering above.
The garden's ecstasy—form, pattern, line—
is much more than precise petal design.
Its particular language, shared by the bee,
is larger than one flower's symmetry.
To bees, a flower is calligraphy
that Nature sketches with economy—
the bee's true genius is design back home—
see the latticework of the honeycomb!

Imprint

Does the monarch carry in its velvety black veins
      the fuzzy black memory of the caterpillar?
Does a lily, its blossoms bursting forth,
      ever reflect on the inner cloister of the bud?
When a frog jumps for the very first time,
      does it forget the blind roaming
           of the tadpole that sees with its tail?

Constructed from dissolved bits of broken caterpillar—
      one histoblast protein cell at a time—
          the monarch knows!
Some small bits of larva brain remain—
      for a butterfly, conditioned as a caterpillar
          to avoid some scents—remembers!—
          and acts the same.
Does the bud live on in the lily?
Does the tadpole bring its knowing to the frog?

Humming: Stalemate

Bird humming, strumming air guitar of wings:
poised obsession—leaving and returning
like a scorned lover burning, yearning.
Absurd surprise—the unheard bird that sings
no song—vibrato of invisible wings brings
no rest—stationed aloft, viewing turning
into elation—motion's love potion churning—
frenzied flutter suspended as it clings.
The flower revels—its scent is spent to lure,
a Buddha dwelling in sun, wind, and shower,
its fragrance broken by commotion,
teasing the bird hovering to endure.
Lady-in-waiting measures out each hour
yet offers up no reverent airborne prayer.

Nightingale

A nightingale sings in an English wood—
his song ever changing and always new.
While he sings day and night as well he should,
his mate, ever mute, never sings on cue.

In the mist and rain, in the fog and dew,
she feels her song as it pulses inside—
if spirit is wind, each horizon new—
her place in the wood is no place to hide.

Nightingale, woman, must improvise—
dance where she can, chase her dream if she would,
following her heart wherever it flies,
finding her way to make jazz in the wood.

NOTE: Though early writers assumed the female nightingale sang, it is in fact the
male, whose song is a loud, whistling crescendo.

In Nautilus Chambers

In nautilus chambers, the moon glows.
How does the shell know what it knows?
Nautilus growth lines mark each day
while chambers number the moon's stay.
As the moon moves, the earth slows.

As the earth moves, the moon shows
itself in ridges, rows on rows,
marking the moon's primordial way
In nautilus chambers.

Nautilus seals itself as it grows,
stows time in logarithmic flows
when a close moon loomed and held sway
and distance led the clock astray,
so the old lunar story goes—
in Nautilus Chambers.

NOTE: The chambered nautilus marks the passage of the moon in growth lines—400 million-year-old nautiloid fossils marked a 21-hour day, a 9-day month and a closer, larger moon, less than half the distance it is from earth today.

Gravity and Size

Gravity is the grand master of size.
Look at the elephant and hummingbird.
Pairing them together may seem absurd.
Still, the elephant walks and the bird flies,
displaying lightweight strength as their disguise.
For creatures this size, time itself is blurred—
The bird's life blinks at the lumbering herd.
Hollow bones, devised for speed, prove wise.
Still, a hummingbird in flight, knows firsthand
though scale may be the story on dry land,
what the bird, flying, like the fish denies:
weightlessness cancels out dimension, size.
Life at sea is all about buoyancy:
gravity does not control the sea.

NOTE: When linear measurements double, surface area quadruples and volume increases by eight—dictating the outer limits of the size of life on land. This law reverses itself in water. The difference is gravity.

NOTE: This drawing by my son Gabriel inspired the following poem.

Root Cause

The Celts, Druids, Pagans, and Witches
      decided to hire a Sleuth.
They gathered together all of their riches
      to pay scholars to rewrite the Truth.

Scouting the future to rewrite the past,
      they knew they had to make haste.
The world could be different—or the die would be cast—
      the Council had no time to waste!

Using all of their cunning and clout
      to undo what all would believe,
the genealogists figured it out—
      they said everything pointed to Eve!

The Sleuth found the trail that led to the tree,
      for the tree was surely to blame.
Do not chop it down, but set the roots free—
      for this tree was the root of man's shame—

Rather, woman, by name. They wanted it all—
      this "treasure" beyond all measure—
for in *her* roots was the cause of it all—
      the sin that had given such pleasure.

Ten archaeologists rooted it out—
      they went way back in time, of course—
and found the Great Tree, beyond all doubt,
      and followed the roots to the source.

They secured the tree's roots in a bathtub hearse—
      the Great Tree that had started it all.
And thereby undid mythology's curse—
      just as the apple was starting to fall!

Turbulence and Stars

In *Starry Night*, Van Gogh's luminous glow
displays movement in air, fluid, and light—
swirling eddies of turbulence in flow—

so art reveals what Science must forego,
conveying much more than the calm of night—
how stars and comets stream luminous glow,

how rivers rill or wisps of smoke will blow.
Van Gogh knew well the turbulence of fright—
its swirling eddies, turbulent in flow.

He saw how currents full of turmoil go
in random swirls—a firefly in flight.
Turbulence has its own luminous glow,

still baffling science with its need to know.
Van Gogh plied brightness to transform our sight—
his brushstrokes—turbulent as eddies flow.

Where science fails, the artist works solo:
this starry night seems ready to ignite—
currents ebb and wane in luminous glow,
swirling eddies of turbulence that flow.

Turbulence

God, Van Gogh and Turbulence

Heisenberg, certain of uncertainty,
petitioned God on Relativity.
Concerning Turbulence, God turned away—
perplexed, then vexed, with even less to say.

Science cannot predict how rapids flow
or how a wafting wisp of smoke will blow
or how air moves around an airplane wing—
here—calculations fail past reckoning.

Van Gogh absorbed the Muse, then let her go;
let eddies, pools of silent pigment flow—
first bright, then dull staccato brushstrokes seem
to pulse, so *Starry Night* appears to gleam.

In pulsing swirls of light, the cosmos stirred.
Like God, abstaining from a single word,
and knowing well the turbulence of fright,
the artist captured awe in whorls of light.

Beyond Hedgerows: Robert Frost and Edward Thomas

One month of English summer, day by day—
a gift of time as way leads on to way—
two friends meandering amid hedgerows
stop to ponder how poetry meets prose.

Biographer and poet go out walking
from Old Fields out past Little Iddens, talking.
Two wordsmiths casting seed, plow lush terrain,
now ripe for carving furrows in the brain.

Together, Frost and Thomas seize the day—
in sun and rain, they keep the world at bay.
They flirt with time to leave the world behind,
to savor—confiscate—fields in the mind.

On Dymock paths they squander time and lose
themselves—enthralled by unexpected views.
As words converge and keep time with footfall,
they pause to ponder cowslips or birdcall.

One day they meet half-way, poised to explore.
The next day, Frost greets Thomas at his door.
As Thomas knows the trees and birds by name,
he cautions Frost: no two days are the same.

Thomas seeks different ways to steal a glance—
he courts the wind—trees bend, birds soar, leaves dance—
so rapt in musing, he has cause to doubt—
is he coming in or going out?

Thomas, a winnower of prose hedgerows—
reviewer of lives by precise words he chose—
discovered he was curious and keen
to glean from Frost poetic truths unseen.

He saw in Frost fresh sensibility
about new paths that lead to poetry.
For newcomer and novice, like these two—
in camaraderie, old paths turned new.

Thomas knows well the path not taken,
a path dismissed, a poem forsaken
for prose, and still he walks the gaps within,
hears Frost find poetry in prose, begin

to notice cadence, breathe the pace of walking,
imbibe the measure, flow and beat of talking.
Then Thomas, grieving at the path they chose,
amuses Frost—is poetry disguise for prose?

Frost stretches out then sketches out his view
on how each may reveal divergent hues—
poised, poem and prose might merge together
in much the way wildflowers meet heather.

Two paths converged in such poignant surprise—
for Thomas, a keen chronicler of lives—
to realize his neighbor was a man
who, at his core, had come to understand

that poetry, possessed by counts and kings,
could, still, instead, portray all sorts of things
a common man might keep at bay, then say
while walking hedgerows on a summer day.

Embracing Thomas like a brother, Frost
would savor time, but not the brutal cost
of ruminating under darkening skies,
while mulling over where poetry lies.

Their random tandem walking soon would end—
a shell at Arras severed friend from friend.
Alone now, Frost wanders between hedgerows,
still wondering how poetry meets prose.
He dwells on loss, aches for one easeful word,
haunted by the voice no longer heard.

Vermeer's Light

The Dutch worked magic—turning sand to glass—
displaying artistry few could surpass.
As Delft glass makers honed an ancient art,
a fledgling science—*Optiks*—got its start.
Fine wired spectacles were everywhere,
their lenses glittering like gems laid bare,
from massive telescopes that scanned the skies
to tiny lenses for the weakest eyes;
spy glasses, monocles in every store,
with peddlers selling eyewear door-to-door.

As artisans and artists shared a guild,
their common ground became a dream fulfilled.
Vermeer's distilled light seemed to cast a spell—
was it the Devil's magic? Who could tell?

Did darkroom magic give Vermeer a clue?
His *camera obscura* changed the view—
though light rays cast an image upside down,
a concave mirror turned the scene around.
If one proved magical, why not try two?
A second mirror might enhance the view.
The image flattened out 3-D to two,
intensifying color's depth and hue.

The color white contains a span of light
in shades invisible to human sight.
If science spied on art, what was the prize?—
Vermeer possessed a second set of eyes!

By viewing a reflected range of hues,
Vermeer could sort the violets and blues.
To his surprise, the mirror helped him see
a complex palette with new clarity.
He'd mix his paint to match the mirror's hue—
when the tones merged, the edge would fade from view.
Techniques like these were rare among the trades
and earned the novice painter accolades.

The painter-sleuth perfected mimicry,
concealing techniques—so like trickery,
inciting cynics to dismiss his muse—
was cleverness fair reason to accuse?

If light conveys the truth, it tells it slant,
and makes it ever harder to recant.
Devising special tools to sharpen sight,
Vermeer captured the subtlety of light
by rendering how shadows leave their mark
as twilight wanes and light is touched by dark.
Vermeer's lens stops the moments as they pass,
distilling years into an hour-glass.

Interstices

The space between is the thing that matters,
How we enter or exit, the pathway itself.
Is it an open doorway with a view?
Or merely a sliver of light squeezed tight by weather stripping,
      worn edges framing a gap that needs closing to keep wind and rain at bay?
At bay, water from below beckons us
     to calm breeze or stormy sky.
One lone table, pen and ink, black journal poised,
pauses in front of the writer's chair facing backwards—
      back to the door, allowing the mind's eye to paint
      the view or write it askew, slanted like the rooftops cast in the sun.
Blue door, gray vase, orange flowers glow in the glass.
Two images—orange blossoms both real and imagined—reflection
      of a moment on the edge
      where one stands on the ledge, deciding
      whether going out or coming in matters most.
Like the space between the spokes,
      the strength of the wheel hinges on nothing—
      the spaces that hold up the spokes,
        he places in between.

Light Dancer

The performer takes his place
        on a silent, dark stage—empty black sky
            for a human constellation,
                for a dancer draped in light.

He built himself a costume of light—miniature flashlights
        strapped to his wrists, forearms, elbows, thighs, ankles,
            even his forehead ringed by a band of light.
                He draws a partner's body with his own.

As he moves, his steps tap out surprise rhythms
        of light and dark—a silent film of swaying limbs,
        elongated, contracting, extending—each movement
            re-configuring space as the dance keeps changing.

Anonymous figures loom—silhouettes pirouette across the wall—
        pretend parade, moving charade of others dancing—a million dancers
        dancing—all moving mysteriously as he moves—in sync
            with the one dancer dancing with light.

He was born into dancing,
        before birth, at birth, from birth
           in that first dark, womb-cocoon
              where he first felt the other dancing.

The muscles remember—tender memories
        of the moving mirror who danced with him—
           arms and legs flying, handstands, flips, jumps,
              laughing with the one who always laughed back.

After laughter, how does he trace a pattern of loneliness?
        How does he dance alone? Devise a new dance without a partner?
    Create a partner in space—with space? How does he confront the dark—
           with an alphabet of light? He draws a partner's body with his own.

A human firefly writing with light,
he dances sublime pantomime
to chase away the dark,
to court his own shadow dancing in the light.

No Object

A tassel-headed oracle bird would speak—
      with its open ceramic beak, yet it stays mute and meek.
A stained glass hummingbird hangs still as stone;
      fixed by the window, it lives alone.
A little brass box even the bard would not claim
      for its misspelling of Shakespear's name.
A cross-legged fiddler makes up a tune
      that will not be heard anytime soon.

The object holds its own,
      suspended animation carved in stone
      or metal or wood; it does not answer to what is good
      or evil, hot or cold, does not behave as one might wish it would.
The object does not care or stare,
      is not invested or tested by our gaze,
      better yet, has no issues to raise.
The object does not engage or enrage,
      has no stake in us; sees no mistake in us.
The object does not attach or attack,
      does not push forward or pull back.
The object asks nothing of us, puts nothing on us,
does not coax us into action or put us in traction,
does not invite and then reject.

Only one object defies the rule and creates its own school
      of possibility—each time it is taken off the shelf,
         it goes beyond itself, coming alive in human hands.
         Its magic combines time
with air, wood, metal, skin, or strings—
      and transforms both time and space,
         as it moves beyond these things.

Whether flute, fiddle, horn or drum, sound rebounds, resounds,
    plays back, recalls itself, resolves itself—reverberating air and vibrating eardrum,
      strumming both tone and that nothingness between tones—
         mystery born from silence.

Notes from Nothing

Music lies in the spaces between—
in that interval, the space the brain craves—
not the similarity between notes
but the difference, the delta, the friction—
invisible steps beckoning up or down.

One tone strikes a chord that opens us;
two tones together startle us to weep.
Music is a tale of two—one note cannot survive
in isolation—each needs the sequence of the next
across the spaces between.

How can so much happen in the silence
of waiting—the crafted pause hanging on,
dangling precariously on the edge
of the next tone? Progress plummets us
from one note to the next,

pulling us down a line, soon stretching us taut—
surprise pizzicato—leaving us shaken—resonating
invisible strings evoking lifetimes,
birthed from moments
of absolute nothing.

The Violinmaker

I

The violinmaker runs her fingers along each groove,
but lets the hours slip through her grasp,
like spruce shavings falling to the floor.
She is the purfling—the ornamental fine line flirting with the edge.
She is both serpentine mouths of the fiddle through which she breathes the world.
She is the surprise asymmetry of the bass bar—main artery of the violin placed askew,
off-center.
She is the sound box, the eggshell-like sounding box housing its own room full of air.
She is the hairline crack in old instruments, the crack between purfling and groove—
the crack that benefits tone, enhances flexibility, makes the fiddle sing.
She is the soundpost—a vertical post of spruce fitted and held in place by friction—
the soul of the violin.
She is the friction between grain and grace, the space between tone and tune.
She is the scroll, the curving wooden question mark.
She is the bridge
She is the bow.
She is the voice.

II

But she is more viola than violin—the underrated,
overlooked stepsister of the violin,
the dark horse of the quartet, subject to no rules
of construction, no set pattern or dimension,
mere accompaniment to the violin—yet
the harmonic center of the quartet.
The viola is never what it seems—
problematic from the start—the brunt of countless jokes,
too small for its tone, too big to play easily—
disturbing the player, pushing the limits
of dimension and convention.
"The quartet is perfection!"
"Why a vertical viola?"
"Why a violin octet?"

Part quartet, part chamber orchestra—
nothing more, nothing less
than a new palette of sound.

III

Of all the energy the player feeds into the violin,
only a tiny bit emerges as sound—the rest escapes as heat.
She is the friction of delta, the solo sound
emerging from the fiddle, soaring
on a current all its own.

Soundpost

Just a small, sturdy, dense column of wood
that does little more than hold up the world.
Unlikely conduit wedged to edges
of carved spruce and maple, this upright post
holds the space between as if sacred.
Wedged not glued in place, a channel for sound
between opposites, top and back held at bay,
connecting nothingness to form a whole,
allowing air currents to swirl inside,
maintaining the ribs of separation.
A conduit, a short circuit between
rocking bridge and box, it amplifies the sound
of bow on string, thus keeping the fiddle
from caving in on itself, air snuffed out
by the sheer force of the bow on the strings.
A minute, invisible inch of wood,
a part of the fiddle hidden from view,
except for those who know to look for it—
maker, player, dealer, or collector—
seeking to adjust the sound with the key:
a vertical post, tall talisman held still
by friction. Without it, the violin
mimics a guitar. The space between
matters most for the conduit across
time and space, between science and art,
linking the two across the great divide,
building a bridge where there had been a wall.
Wedged between two worlds, yet glued to neither,
still able to move, to change position,
jockey for space or make an adjustment.
One tiny move can make the most difference,
the space between a hush or rush of wind,
a single post poised in the space between,
finding the perfect resting place somewhere
inside the crevice that cradles the sound.

NOTE: First published in *American Luthier: Carleen Hutchins—the Art and Science of the Violin* (ForeEdge, 2016), selected by PEN America as one of Ten Best Biographies of 2017.

Black Hole

When a thousand moments crystallize
into one, and the snow globe you know
flips all on its own in one mute moment,
familiar landscapes simply disappear.
The outer world crushes the inner world—
and splinters into a million sharp shards
that suddenly collapse, disparate bits
sucked inward—mass imploding on itself—
a dense black hole fused into one vacuum—
the gravitational pull of love and loss.
Nothing known stays, save for the need to breathe—
the inescapable airlessness of grief.
Time floats; silent horizons freeze the days.
Snail-like, the world moves in a grain of sand.

Onion Moon

Even as clouds form, they race across the sky.
A flower blooms as it prepares to die.
The bee that hovers only seems to stay.
The monarch lights, dazzles, then flies away.
The woodpecker stops short his hollow ring
just in time for the meadowlark to sing.
Her melody is lost amidst the trees
where gold leaves wrestle an incessant breeze.
The constant motion of a summer's day
becomes night's onion moon and peels away.
Nature's creatures dart, then flit out of sight.
You, too! You left too soon—like October light.
Since your death, time—and life—move in reverse.
Nature, help me forgive the universe.

Tug-of-War

Birdwatcher

She stands stooped, binoculars hanging,
peering through glasses through a telescope
aimed at the horizon, determined to get the best sighting.

Gazing through three different lenses, deciphering
fog and sky, sky and shoreline, shore and wave,
sand and bird—sandpiper, cormorant, gull, and tern.

A tricky endeavor—to move too soon
between wind and feather, telescope eye focused on lens,
the other eye squinting to keep from seeing double.

With binoculars, both eyes merge the view—a single turn
renders the world anew as lens moves bird from far to near—
mottled, speckled design flitting across sand. Still, each lens

gives back the quandary of reflection—an image
of herself—but for her, only a distraction
from real seeing. I am the birdwatcher

and the bird, watching my own life from the air,
chasing the speck with spectacles, a moving blur
with binoculars—trying to merge twin sightings—

Aerial View

You are water; I am earth.
You, nestled in a salt-soaked cabin floating under starlit canopies.
I, a world away, watching the gurgling wooded stream that borders a backyard
    turret,
my shingled observation deck nestled in trees.

I watch a blue jay flit from branch to branch
and imagine the buoyancy of flight.
You live buoyancy, studying the seagull's swoop while holding tight to ropes,
standing firm against the rhythmic rocking of the floor beneath your feet.

The birds give us airy common ground—their cross-hatch web
of flight patterns, a frenzied backdrop for woods or wharf.
Birds connect us over land or water—over what we cannot see
of the other's world.

The hawk keeps vigil atop his solitary outpost;
the blue heron forms his own perch—one pencil leg down,
the other hidden from view.
Both are silent statues, scanning.

Then suddenly these still observers rush away,
take flight. They know the journey better than the destination,
planning on the wing, trusting wind and current;
they chart the next move by making it.

Mining inner radar, soaring through the silence of distance,
two like birds find each other, join the syncopated flock. Difference matters little
when the journey is the destination. With grit and grace,
they find the future by not clinging to it.

Going First

For nine months we swam
in warm darkness, sparring swimmers,
prodding, poking one another,
chasing each other in circles,
primal partners,
cloistered in darkness,
forever linked by blood
and the sanctuary of shared space.

Freed from the confines of sight,
suspended in weightlessness, we danced
in tandem, not knowing. As if choreographed
to some pre-ordained, unplayed tune, improvised
with rhythms we could not name, the dance slowed.
As the lake began to shrink,
we found our positions blindly,
sensing each other.

As pressure swelled, a speck of light appeared.
Poised in sightless seeing, we pretended
not to notice, but the irresistible light grew larger,
brighter, until it seemed to engulf me,
wooing me away from you.
Drawn to it, but sensing separation, I lingered,
reluctant to sever the invisible tether
of our connection.

Then some curious movement
sent me tunneling down on pioneer passage,
like an astronaut flying through the aurora borealis,
defying gravity yet landing softly,
caught in a gentle grasp, stunned
by a world of light, noise, mystery.
Alone in blinding light, I wondered
where the darkness had taken you.

Moon Chaser's Musing

Are worlds built around the memory
of a moment?
Did I choose to chase the moon?
Did you choose to watch?
Choice matters little next to the way
pattern became our lives.

For the moon chaser
who risks the journey
through the sky that beckons
like the stars, the horizon is filled
with possibility, life propelled
by forward thrust. Curiosity
and exhilaration catapult
the sky traveler upward, outward,
thrust from doubt into daring
by the pull of light.

For the star gazer who watches
lost light flicker in the distance,
departure leaves its mark. Losing sight
of the sky traveler in empty sky
calls into memory the irrevocable fact
that sight cannot contain all,
that two cannot fly in one orbit.
Waiting for return becomes yearning
that amplifies doubt, raising questions
the first sky traveler never knew.

While the one who goes first
leaves history behind,
the one who stays
guards a memory.

Minutes Apart

What is it like to share the first day,
the birth day, with someone
who was as much there as you,
only minutes from you?

Years after sameness has glued you together,
or strangeness has unglued you forever,
the candles that burn are never yours, or mine.
The hours of that day remain ours.

After years of prayers for imaginary encounters,
after forgiveness and forgetting has begun to mend
the broken wall, the unending question of the birth day
rises up like smoke from snuffed-out candles.

The lights go down; the song begins.
I sing for you, so long ago gone into time.
I hear your voice next to mine.
Our birthday burns again.

It is like standing at the starting gate
of a race you will run shoulder to shoulder,
only minutes apart, keeping pace
with the one only minutes away.

But the race begins,
no partner shows,
so you run with your hand
dragging in the wind.

Epiphany

It was a fifth-grade playground prank
with all the larger-than-life proportions
of youth theater. On the same field
where heroics of soccer and football
assume the magnitude of Roman gladiators,
here, the plan began,
the plan to make the switch.

We had switched many times before:
to avoid someone, to pretend for one
so the other could escape.
But now, the big test:
Could we play the game
for a whole day
without the teachers ever knowing?

Amid snickers and the sheer ecstasy
of fifth-grade prank playing,
they never knew. They got the joke,
but not. The best theater is too good, too real.
Our theater was so good, it left the stage,
hovering somewhere
above the audience.

Our story got good press,
lasting for weeks, lingering
in the glints of teachers' eyes, rippling
across the muddy waters of our days,
echoing encores in the cathedrals of our minds,
to play over again without
the relief of applause.

Time stood still that afternoon
when we first saw the illusion
of ourselves. While everyone laughed
and retold our story, we walked home
in deepening silence.
Without words,
we put the game to rest.

No Laughing Matter

We knew each other's shoes too well
to step outside our own, and then,
wishing to flee another's spell
caused us to journey further still.

Our skin was much too much for us,
like a shadow or a cloak.
To stretch past silhouette, we drew
two lines 'round what we knew we knew.

We wandered still our double maze,
a house of mirrors penny arcade
where images danced in a fun house—
but where had all the laughter gone?

While listening so hard to name
the tunes we heard within,
we did not hear the melodies
that played beyond our skin.

We could not find the way to laugh,
to step outside our skin.
We could not step outside our world
to let the laughter in.

Illusion

Two profiles, face to face,
are twins to each other.
Then facing profiles are twin
to the chalice between profiles—
the eye floats back and forth
between profiles
and chalice.

The first illusion is the doubling—
mirror images
looking at each other.
The second illusion is more elusive,
as profiles seem to move towards chalice
and chalice explodes back
into profiles.

The Middle English verb for *"to twin"*
means to split or divide—but the old adage
"we twa will never twin" means "we will never part."
To split apart or to join together?
Twin means both—
like the optical illusion
of facing profiles.

Release

I did not know I took from you
the words to say your peace.
I did not know I stole away
the means for your release.

I did not know my words
imprisoned you in silence.
I did not know your private rage
as I began to take the stage.

How could I know in silent night
the terror that I wrought—
I became the word
while you were never heard.

How could I know?
You never told me so—
and mine was not
to wonder why.

And so we lived, wrapped in a lie—
that we were friend and friend,
the lie that I would live
and you pretend

until a time when distance
set you free,
no longer plagued
by thoughts of me.

Yours was a high price to pay—
a lifetime spent looking away.

Questions for a Kid Sister

The faded photograph of you, age four—
Why does this view of you surprise me so?
Your flowered dress reminds me of the days
of double hand-me-downs that you would wear.

You took your own amazement everywhere.
Four years young, you arrived in your own time
and made the best of it—or maybe not—
you never knew a time before the twins.

You always kept them open—doors and ears.
You never judged, or took sides, but kept peace—
made room for us when we had none for you;
loved us although we had no time for you.

We never saw you tapping on the wall
of our glass house. How did togetherness
become a shield, a weapon we would wield
without foreseeing that the loss was ours?

Tug-of-War

In tug-of-war, players
must be partners in pulling.
If one gives way, the other collapses.
To connect means to maintain tension.

Few can risk the tightrope
of relationship without two
lassoed trees, equally strong,
tested over time.

You chose the tensile strength
of silence; I grabbed at slack words.
Can you string a rope of words
across rushing torrents of emotion?

It takes two to make it taut,
whether it is a rope to walk,
or a line on which to hang
feelings out to dry.

You pull away, repulsed
by the volume of my words.
I hold on, stranded
by the vacuum of your silence.

Will the rope hold evenly
for partners in pulling,
or will it fray and give way,
yanking one of us over the river's edge?

Traveling Light

She travels light, a knapsack on her back.
In her house, objects must be tied to teak or float away.
Her mailbox is a mooring.
Though she can leave land each day,
she cannot leave her thoughts.
Swaying like her boat house,
she wavers between thoughts she cannot leave
and things she will not see. Or maybe she takes with her
only thoughts of the next horizon.
Feelings hover, like buoys bobbing,
or weigh her down like a loose anchor adrift
or a mock mooring tethering her through a storm.

Her sister climbs a hill on moving day,
carrying box after box of objects meant for windowsills
and mantelpieces, her mind adrift. Needlepoint cushions,
photo albums, picture frames, lifetimes of cloistered clutter,
memories sequestered by wood, brick and mortar
now filling the boxes that fill her arms,
boxes in the attic, boxes in the basement,
boxes she would rather move than sort.
But she has sorted other things that know no shape or size.
She has carried thoughts many miles, until looking at them
has made her put her baggage down. Unlike the boxes
she carries up the hill, her thoughts get lighter as she moves.

Star Drawings

Is silence turbulence, prayer,
or the music of forgetting?

Is silence invisible waves of knowing,
the whipping of wind, vibration without sound,
except as it thrashes things,
a churning, yearning locomotion of longing?

Is silence hypnotic mantra,
centering trance, buoyant benediction,
hope chanting, wakeful listening,
or simply a waiting for the passage of pain?

Is silence the drumbeat
for beating down thought,
a song sung louder than memory,
rereading memory's melody with new notations?

Is silence peace, or a void
of numbing nothingness, a tunneling down darkness
too deep to acknowledge,
or a vast rest from pondering anything?

I scan the night sky for moonlight mask,
shooting star, aurora to grasp
the silent language of star drawings.
I wonder if silence works like words,
if it has a substance of its own,
a winding windsong of pictures,
symbols, signs soaring like shooting stars,
images gone as fast as they appear—
a mesmerizing mural that lingers.

Vanishing Point

With its daily turbulence—eddies,
currents, whirlpools—swirling beneath
the salty froth of crashing waves, the sea emerges.
Anonymous swells disappear in fast foam
or vanishing wake as the boat splits the water,
a moving island bordered by teak,
rope, sail and sheeting, its path
disappearing as soon as it forms.

The sailor, content to lose sight
of land in the simpler line
of the horizon, roams a watery floor
ever moving, aiming the sail,
alternating between facing into the wind
and turning away, changing
direction with the will
of the wind.

Voices trail off, missed words lost
in the rush of wind—conversations
can simply float away.
Weather matters most.
No trespassing. Isolated by wind
and water, sea neighbors
are easy to avoid, protectors
of parched privacy.

Does brittle memory fade easily,
or simply wear away over time,
peeling back in layers
like familiar letters
on the side of a boat, nearly gone
from fighting sun, salt, barnacle?
The sea is bigger
than memory.

Still, can the sailor escape the silent salt scent
of memory, pungent as beached seaweed
that lingers in the air,
clinging to the docks?

Trading Words

I spoke without warning
on the first morning of words.
My words filled the air,
beginning our story,
amplified by your mute consent.

Each word drew us
into the current of a swift stream
where faces were only reflections,
and echoes easily mistaken
for voices.

Teasing my ear like an unanswered breeze,
your silence pulled us downstream
as the deafening rush of water drowned
the sounds of two voices merging
into one swirling whirlpool of words.

For you, whose first unfurled language
was silence, words must seem both precious
and cheap, like colored pebbles lying in a stream,
shining with wet sparkle, pristine,
a lost primal currency.

Would that we could trade words
as the Aborigines traded stones, counting them
with measured precision, examining each for defects,
allowing others to fall through our hands
to the forgiving stream, anointing our waiting feet.

Declaration

She was the morning when silence took its stand.
She was the storm that never materialized.
She was the card game where no one showed her hand.
She was the party that never happened.
She was the music that played beyond me.
She was the fight where only one showed up.
She was the laughter I never heard.
She was the river that rushed to the falls.
She was the dream of the Ferris wheel that never stopped.
She was the bag filled with things I should have done.
She was the reason I found my voice.

Mind Map

Stepping away from a twin
is like stepping out of a dream
that has shrouded you
from the day you were born.
For the willful pioneer,
the journey begins with a jolt.
The air is different, the sounds new.
There are no familiar landmarks—
this learning how to be
without belonging.

If and when some small inner voice
asks not to be confused with someone else,
seeking self means choosing not to belong.
Instead of running towards home,
we must run away from what we know best.
Though we all live in different stages
of awakening, twins must emerge
from the deepest sleep, and even then,
never quite lose that haunting sensation
of being somehow incomplete.

Redemption

The road home
is neither straight nor narrow.
Detours distract,
      tangents tempt,
          wandering off
      into uncharted territory,
as way leads on to way.

Finding your way back
      to some primal direction
         means walking the path,
wherever it leads.

What begins as unattended hedgerows
      on a country lane, grows wild
with time and neglect
until the jungle encircles you,
overgrown high and thick—
      swallowing horizons.

Over time, the path becomes
a labyrinth folding back on itself.
The only way out is forward motion
      aimed at the horizon, the next moment, a new day—the unknown.

The greatest risk is not the obstacle in the path—
      the stone, the boulder, or even the ledge ahead,
         but instead, the riveting way that old paths
     invite us home, calling old selves by name, wooing us
back, urging us to remember that the path of least resistance
      is the familiar one—despite the fact that risk
     is hidden everywhere, mostly in mines masked as signposts—
         repeating patterns that keep us lost.

Choice alone finds the route.
We grow sane by paying attention to the journey—
not rehearsing it, nursing it, or even cursing it but listening to it,
        plowing through it, carving a path through the thicket
                of experience to understand
        how we came to this moment,
                what this moment holds,
                        where it points as it unfolds.

Tattoo

Tandem, twins
flaunt and taunt
the unity
of two.

Still, a pair, pared down
to one, leaves a mark—
as public persona dissolves
into a singular portrait.

Twin tattoo turns inward—
invisible imprint—
indelible ink
inside.

The invisibility of duality
and oneness leaves its own residue,
seeping inside as self hides
behind a curtain of solitude.

Togetherness is as tangible
as invisibility—both are real—
whether or not the partner
is visible.

The nature of separation is its own puzzle—
absence has its own presence,
a voice with an undetectable
volume all its own.

What color is the skin of a twin?
The color of water after spring rains,
when reflecting pools
hold all the colors at once.

Like twinship,
color is its own illusion—nothing
but reflection at different frequencies—
even the blue sky is its own lie.

There would be no blue sky without the eye—
perception creates color. Likewise, perception
peers past tattoo—
or clings to it.

So what color is the twin
standing alone without her partner—
without the protection
of reflection?

What happens to light without darkness?
What clings to the surface of water
when reflections are gone?
What color is water at night?

The Wax Tablet

We are hard-wired to each other,
never tethered to the world.
The only evidence of shared place
is placenta, soon replaced
by intangible umbilical cords
that tie us together
beyond birth.

My memory is a wax tablet.
Each time I lift the plastic sheet
to clean the slate, I start again
to lift the fog in my mind
so that I may read the message
you left behind about where
to look for memory.

To My Brother

Though first-born to my twin, I was not first-born.
My brother, three years young, you stood by, stunned
by a double arrival that signaled a challenge to your survival,
not because love diminished but because its embrace
loosened to include two more.

It was like the door latched behind you—
the doorknob, too high for you to reach,
so you could only look through the keyhole,
wishing you could climb back through
to the time before we knew you.

Instead, the key turned,
locking out the past—
as our twinship ensnared you, scared you,
pared you down and stared you down,
dared you to be as big as two.

What singleton can compete with two sets
of identical feet, miles of smiles, charade
and parade of fanfare? Still now, as I look down
an arcane arcade of memories you do not share,
I peer deep into the past to see you, at last.

I marvel at my own myopia, at how long
it has taken me to see the cloud that still shrouds
my view of you. So many years later,
I struggle to make my way through twin thickets
to see you standing there.

You and I

You tell yourself you can be free
in salty anonymity.
Unsure about which way to go,
you take the path you do not know.
To lose yourself in wind and rain,
to keep from going home again,
you make your home in wake and foam—
you'd rather float, or maybe roam.
A houseboat is your sparse abode,
with objects tied to teak, or stowed.
Horizon is a simpler line
to lose the past you left behind.

*

On moving day I climb the hill,
my things meant for a windowsill.
I carry boxes one by one—
my remnants of a time undone.
Now objects take me back in time
to moments golden and sublime;
remembering makes the spirit sing—
for stories cling to everything.

*

Horizon is this monster hill:
of sorting things, I've had my fill.
I often wonder how I bring
an addled brain to everything
about you—so much angst I've found
I soon must put my baggage down.
Sometimes I think I must explore
beyond the threshold of this door.
I wonder how it is at sea.
Is each day an eternity?
And as for time—where does it go?
Is it friend or is it foe?

Letter to Myself

The corridor of love is extra wide—
strewed nuggets of forgiveness side to side.
We need not court the dark that draws us in
or let ourselves be driven mad by din.
We could leave our baggage at the door—
and with it, all the blame we have in store.
Choose light and not the gnawing need to know—
the key to understanding is "let go."
By judging less, we suddenly see more:
what is could be much better than before.
To see each other with an angled view
leaves each the room in which to see anew.

A former *Boston Globe* arts journalist, **Quincy Whitney** is a Metropolitan Museum of Art Research Fellow; an award-winning biographer and columnist. *American Luthier*, selected by PEN America as One of Ten Best Biographies of 2017, was awarded the 2019 Acoustical Society of America Science Communication Award. Whitney is also co-author of *Luminosity: The Self-Healing Light in You* (2020) with Dr. Shirley Snow. *TURBULENCE* is her first book of poetry.

CPSIA information can be obtained
at www.ICGtesting.com
Printed in the USA
LVHW052035140920
665908LV00007B/8